EAST MIDLANDS TRACTION

Andrew Walker

AMBERLEY

First published 2017

Amberley Publishing
The Hill, Stroud
Gloucestershire, GL5 4EP

www.amberley-books.com

Copyright © Andrew Walker, 2017

The right of Andrew Walker to be identified as
the Author of this work has been asserted in
accordance with the Copyrights, Designs and
Patents Act 1988.

ISBN 978 1 4456 6388 3 (print)
ISBN 978 1 4456 6389 0 (ebook)

British Library Cataloguing in Publication Data.
A catalogue record for this book is available from
the British Library.

Typesetting by Amberley Publishing.
Printed in the UK.

Introduction

I grew up in South Yorkshire and, after discovering railway photography in 1978, spent the next few years capturing BR operations in the area that is bounded more or less by York in the north, Doncaster in the east, Sheffield in the south and Manchester in the west – including the Woodhead route in its twilight days. By 1985 I was living in Lincoln, where my proximity to the city's Central station enabled regular visits to capture much of the varied activity there, with occasional forays to the further reaches of the county. My recollection is that Class 31s were dominant back then, with pairs of Type 2s appearing on bulk oil turns and individual locomotives routinely appearing on Royal Mail and engineering work. A visit to Central station most evenings would reveal at least one 31, and sometimes up to four, stabled in the bay platforms at the eastern end of the station. Class 37s, 47s, DMUs and HSTs added to the mix, while the first generation Sprinters were making their presence felt. I left Lincoln after two years and moved to Nottingham, close to the main line out of the city through Beeston to Trent Junction, and the variety of motive power on offer was further enhanced, particularly as Toton depot was now on the doorstep. This was a time of change, as the numbers of operational Class 20s and 45s began to dwindle, and even the Class 56s, which I then thought of as still quite 'new', started to suffer withdrawals from the ranks. The Class 58s, however, were at full complement and, not long afterwards, there was a new kid on the block in the form of the Loughborough-built Brush Class 60. The Midland Main Line also offered the scope to capture on film a diverse range of cross-country freight and passenger operations through Derby, which remains a key hub to this day.

Geographically, the East Midlands are, of course, a very extensive area of England, and it would be beyond the scope of this book to deliver comprehensive coverage, meaning that there are inevitably omissions. However, my aim is to present a pictorial volume that contains an illustrative and diverse cross section of both 'vintage' and new material, which I hope will feature something to absorb and interest all readers. My thanks go to fellow photographers John Walker and Vaughan Hellam, who generously contributed some excellent images from their own collections, particularly from those important transitional years of the 1980s. Many of these depict locomotives and infrastructure that has, of course, now gone forever.

Andrew Walker
Nottingham, 2016

Acknowledgements

The author and publisher would like to thank John Walker and Vaughan Hellam for permission to use copyright material in this book. All other photographs are by the author.

Magnificent backdrop for No. 31203

With the towering bulk of the cathedral dominating the skyline, Brush Type 2 No. 31203 takes a rest at Lincoln Central in the summer of 1987. At this time No. 31203 was one of an increasing number of Class 31s beginning to appear in 'large logo' grey-and-yellow livery.

Railfreight livery for No. 31243

Sporting a relatively recent change of livery from rail blue to 'large logo' grey and yellow, otherwise known as Railfreight grey, No. 31243 stands in sub-zero temperatures at Lincoln in January 1986. This bay platform was the usual location for stabling any visiting Type 2s.

Sleaford departure at Lincoln Central

The old order is represented here at Lincoln Central on a bright but chilly February day in 1986. A two-car Cravens DMU waits to depart for Sleaford while station pilot No. 08102 stands in its usual place in one of the bays.

No. 08102 stabled at Lincoln Central

A portrait of Lincoln's long-serving station pilot No. 08102, seen here stabled in one of the bay platforms at Central station in January 1986. This locomotive was routinely used for marshalling Royal Mail stock. By 1989 it had been repainted in green livery as D3167 and used as a static exhibit at Lincoln, but later found productive use once more on the Lincolnshire Wolds Railway.

General manager's saloon at Lincoln Central

This two-car Gloucester RCW unit was converted for use as the Eastern Region general manager's saloon and renumbered as TDB975539 and No. 975349. Here it is seen in the bay at Lincoln Central in May 1987, in the company of Class 31 No. 31411.

Craven DMU at Lincoln Central

Introduced in 1958, and therefore not quite thirty years old in this picture, a two-car Cravens DMU stands at Lincoln in the evening sunshine in April 1987. The leading car is Motor Brake Second No. 51299, with Driving Trailer Composite No. 56429 behind. When new it presumably had two windscreen wipers.

Passenger duty for new Class 58

Doncaster-built Class 58 No. 58007 is seen here on its first passenger outing, taking Hertfordshire Railtours' 'Midland Macedoine' through Whaley Bridge in September 1984. This locomotive was relatively new at the time, having been completed at the 'plant' in 1983. It later carried out cross-Channel duties in France.

The last of the Skegness whistlers

The very last Class 40-hauled service from Manchester to Skegness ran on Saturday 15 September 1984, and here No. 40181 performs the honours, speeding through Bamford on the Hope Valley route – next stop Sheffield.

New lease of life for English Electric Type 1

With its nameplate commemorating the founder of the Hope cement works, veteran Bo-Bo No. 20168 *Sir George Earle* stands in the factory complex during the open day in September 2005. The Class 20 later appeared in white-and-green livery, and more recently was re-numbered simply as '2' in pale grey paintwork with purple solebar. (J. M. Walker)

Pristine setting for Hope open day visitors

Looking almost impossibly neat and tidy, the cement works at Hope, in the Peak District, plays host to a visiting ensemble of steam and diesel for the open day celebrations of September 2008. Class 08 shunter No. 08892 is sharing shuttle duties with a veteran L&Y 0-6-0 tender locomotive. (J. M. Walker)

Pelham Street Junction, Lincoln

Looking east from Lincoln's Pelham Bridge, a trio of empty two-car DMUs approaches the station from the Market Rasen direction while, on the right, departmental unit Nos 975664 and 975637, known as the 'Stourton Saloon', stands outside the depot.

Class 47 on Norsk Hydro fertiliser

Class 47 No. 47049 is seen here approaching East Holmes at Lincoln with a westbound Norsk Hydro fertiliser working in June 1987. This Brush Type 4 was later re-liveried in Railfreight Distribution colours but by 1999 was out of service and stripped for spares at Wigan Springs Branch.

Earles Sidings panorama

In an era of lesser vegetation growth, the gloriously rural setting of Earles Sidings at Hope can be better appreciated from this vantage point to the west of the compact yard. As a Class 158 Sprinter unit passes on the main line, a Class 37 prepares to depart on a light engine move after depositing wagons in April 1995. (J. M. Walker)

Snowy Cromptons on the Hope Valley

Pristine snow lies on the Derbyshire hills as Class 33s Nos 33116 *Hertfordshire Railtours* and 33025 *Sultan* head 'The Gladstone Bag' railtour through Edale in January 1995. The tour had started out with Class 47 haulage at Swindon and visited Liverpool before completing its itinerary at Bristol Temple Meads. (J. M. Walker)

HST approaches Blankney crossing, Metheringham

A cold and bright winter Sunday in 1987 sees HST power car No. 43047 leading a diverted King's Cross–Newcastle service on the approach to Metheringham station, on the Sleaford–Lincoln route. The train will travel via Gainsborough to re-join the East Coast Main Line at Doncaster.

Approaching Saxilby's semaphores

The fine lattice-post bracket semaphore signal at Saxilby is soon to lose its secondary arm as track rationalisation looms in the winter of 1987; in this view, an HST is caught approaching the station from the Gainsborough direction with a diverted Sunday King's Cross service.

No. 31441 on the TPO at Newark

Class 31 No. 31441 brings the evening Travelling Post Office service past the former goods warehouse and into Newark Castle station, where it will stop to take on more mail before departing for Nottingham and ultimately, Crewe. The date was 16 June 1987.

Full power on for No. 58010 at Worksop

In the summer of 1998, Class 58 No. 58010 works hard to shift its loaded MGR train up grade from Shireoaks to Worksop. The destination will be either West Burton or Cottam power station, both of which lie to the east of Retford, around 15 miles or so from here.

Type 2 on freight at New Mills South

The Class 25 fleet was approaching the twilight of its life when this tidy-looking example, No. 25323, was caught heading a westbound train of cargo vans towards New Mills South Junction in August 1984. (V. Hellam)

Tinsley Peak on Hope Valley cement

Class 45 No. 45022 was something of a celebrity among Tinsley's allocation by the summer of 1984, and the Type 4 veteran had been specially treated with white buffers and window frames when it was pictured passing Chinley with a cement working on 31 August. (J. M. Walker)

No. 25302 on ICI hoppers

The track layout around Chinley had not yet been remodelled when Class 25 No. 25302 was captured heading for Peak Forest with a rake of classic ICI hoppers in September 1981. The telegraph wires add to a period feel, despite the absence of semaphore signals. (V. Hellam)

No. 66132 on Dowlow to Southampton aggregates service

Still carrying its original EWS maroon-and-yellow livery, No. 66132 is seen here taking a heavily loaded train of aggregates through Buxworth on the Hope Valley route, destined for Southampton. The bright red box-style open wagons are becoming ubiquitous on the national network.

No. 47352 opens up on ballast at Duffield

Around 5 miles north of Derby on the main line to Chesterfield, No. 47352 cranks up the power at Duffield while working a loaded ballast train in June 1988. The train is just passing the connection with the Wirksworth freight branch, which after closure became the Ecclesbourne Valley Railway and still has a connection to the national network here.

No. 31290 goes north at Clay Cross

The Midland Main Line divides at Clay Cross, with the line to Nottingham via the Erewash Valley diverging from the Derby route. In this image, Class 31 No. 31290 heads north off the former line with a summer service from Yarmouth to Leeds in June 1983. (J. M. Walker)

Westhouses panorama

A forest of yard lamps surrounds the occupants of Westhouses depot near Alfreton in June 1983. The Class 56s and 20s 'on shed' in this view will probably be Toton-based locomotives. The closure of the Nottinghamshire collieries spelled the end for characterful depots like this one. (J. M. Walker)

Shirebrook stabling point for No. 58032

Another long-closed East Midlands depot, Shirebrook was a routine stabling location for the Class 58s between their colliery to power station turns. Here No. 58032 has just arrived 'on shed' in September 1992. This Doncaster-built Type 5 was only seven years old at the time of this picture, but was withdrawn just eight years later. It was subsequently exported to France. (J. M. Walker)

No. 37084 goes west at New Mills South

Class 37 No. 37084 heads onto the Stockport lines at New Mills South Junction with a heavily loaded aggregates service from Peak Forest on a rather overcast 31 August 1984. This locomotive later became No. 37718 and survived until 2015, being cut up at Rotherham. (V. Hellam)

Three-car DMU at Whaley Bridge

A Sunday service from Buxton to Manchester Piccadilly slows for its stop at Whaley Bridge in the summer of 1984. These DMUs would soon enter the twilight of their careers.

DMU arrival at Lincoln

A bright and frosty March morning in 1986 sees a two-car DMU roll across Lincoln's High Street level crossing and into the station with a service from Sheffield. Beyond the office block, the signalbox at East Holmes can be seen.

Busy Lincoln panorama

This view of Lincoln station in May 1987 reveals no fewer than five types of traction, with Classes 08, 31 and 37 visible, as well as one of the newly introduced Sprinters on the far left, as a two-car DMU departs with a Sleaford service.

Savouring Class 40 power at Worksop

The Class 40s were great favourites on the summer Saturday passenger services to holiday destinations and attracted a loyal following of haulage fans. Here No. 40082 makes a dramatic exit from Worksop station on its way to the east coast in June 1984. (J. M. Walker)

Piccadilly to Skegness with No. 40129

As the summer of 1983 draws to a close on 3 September, Class 40 No. 40129 pulls into Worksop station with a Saturday service from Manchester to Skegness, a diagram that regularly featured the English Electric Type 4. (J. M. Walker)

Hoppers return from Northwich

Class 25s were staple power for the Tunstead–Northwich aggregates circuit in the 1970s and 80s, and here No. 25287 heads towards Chinley with a returning rake of empties in April 1983. The train will take the Peak Forest line at Chinley North Junction. (V. Hellam)

Peak power at Peak Forest

Even with a Class 37 providing banking assistance, Peak No. 45058 has to work hard to shift its loaded aggregates hoppers up the grade from Tunstead at Peak Forest Sidings in this powerful image from August 1985. Another Class 45 prepares to depart on the right. (J. M. Walker)

DMU in the Peak

Once such a common sight across the network, a two-car Metro-Cammell DMU, by now carrying the 'heritage' name tag, departs Edale on the Hope Valley route in April 2000, bound for Manchester Piccadilly.

Busy scene at Earles Sidings

There is standing room only in the yard alongside the Hope Valley route at Earles Sidings, where the short branch to Hope cement works diverges, in this May 2007 view. Freightliner's Class 66 No. 66602 prepares to bring out a loaded train, while another pair of 66s drifts by light engine on the main line. (J. M. Walker)

DMU departure at Saxilby

The semaphore signals are clinging on – just – in this 1987 view of Saxilby station, where the goods loop has recently been severed and the associated signal arm removed. A two-car DMU departs with a Lincoln–Sheffield service – next stop Gainsborough.

Modified HST heads north at Retford

A number of InterCity 125 power cars were modified in the late 1980s, appearing with conventional buffers and push-pull capability in the manner of a Driving Van Trailer. One such example, in InterCity 'Swallow' livery and with full yellow ends, is seen going north at Retford in the summer of 1989.

No. 31411 stabled at Lincoln Central

Carrying its distinctive white stripe, which once extended across the doors and cab sides, Class 31/4 No. 31411 stands in one of Lincoln's bay platforms in May 1987. Later re-liveried in grey, this Type 2 was scrapped in 2005.

HST among the semaphores at Lincoln

An InterCity 125 service from London King's Cross pulls into Lincoln Central station on a bright morning in March 1986. The semaphore signals here have all been replaced with colour lights.

Damp arrival at Chapel-en-le-Frith for Class 150 Sprinter

A rather damp afternoon at Chapel-en-le-Frith sees Class 150 Sprinter No. 150146 pulling into the station with a Buxton–Manchester service in June 1993. The signalbox here was built to a BR standard design with twenty levers, and dates from 1957.

Contrasting front ends at Buxton

Buxton's 'Sandite' diesel unit ADB977554, a former Class 104 DMU, rests at its home base in September 1992, with Tinsley's No. 37684, in Railfreight aggregates livery, also taking a break on the depot sidings behind. Previously No. 37134, this locomotive was scrapped in 2010. The Sandite car, however, survived to enter preservation.

Large logo 50 at Chesterfield

It was relatively common to see Western Region Class 50s operating over the Midland Main Line in the 1980s, following repair or overhaul at Doncaster. Here, No. 50036 *Victorious* draws into Chesterfield with a southbound passenger service in August 1983. This locomotive was fully refurbished at the 'plant' in 1986. (J. M. Walker)

No. 47552 takes Pullman stock south, Clay Cross

The Midland Main Line does not really have the equivalent of the East Coast's 'racetrack' sections, but it has seen engineering improvements to lift the line speed over the years, and here, at Clay Cross, south of Chesterfield, Class 47 No. 47552 is well into its stride with a train of vintage Pullman stock in the summer of 1987. The Erewash Valley line to Nottingham diverges here. (J. M. Walker)

No. 47137 heads west at Lincoln Central

Evening sunshine illuminates Class 47 No. 47137 on 23 April 1987 as it heads west on the centre road at Lincoln Central with what looks like empty fly ash hoppers returning to West Burton power station near Retford. On the left, a two-car DMU has just arrived from Sheffield.

Arrivals and departures at Lincoln

Lincoln station in 1986, and Class 150 Sprinter No. 150129 awaits departure with a service for Crewe via Nottingham and Derby, while an HST has just arrived at Platform 1 with a service from London King's Cross.

Class 58 passes the new Shirebrook station

The new 'Robin Hood Line' station at Shirebrook is not yet open to passengers as Class 58 No. 58041 *Ratcliffe Power Station* passes with a northbound MGR service in March 1998. The original station here closed in 1964.

Early Peak on classic mixed freight

The Midland Main Line north of Chesterfield splits at Tapton Junction, with the 'Old Road' diverging from the direct Sheffield route and heading in a north-easterly direction towards Barrow Hill and Tinsley. Here No. 44007 *Ingleborough* snakes across to the Down slow lines in readiness to take the latter route with this mixed freight in October 1979.

Lincolnshire diversion, 1987

Caught between the telegraph poles, Class 47 No. 47587 disturbs the tranquillity of the Lincolnshire countryside at Metheringham with a diverted East Coast service in March 1987. Judging from the rather odd mix of coaching stock, this could well be a relief working.

No. 47634 on East Coast diversion

Trains on the East Coast Main Line were diverted through Lincoln over the weekend of 26/27 January 1986. Seen here with one of the northbound workings, No. 47634 *Henry Ford* passes Pelham Street Junction signalbox. Later named *Holbeck*, No. 47634 was scrapped after suffering generator damage in 2001. The signalbox lasted a little longer, being closed in 2008.

Nos 20168 and 20059 approach Bilsthorpe colliery

Bilsthorpe was one of the easternmost collieries in the Nottinghamshire coalfield. In this image from June 1992, a passenger special approaches from the Clipstone direction with Class 20s Nos 20168 and 20059 in charge. Another pair is bringing up the rear and will lead the train back out after reversal under the colliery loading bunker.

Mainline's No. 60088 at Shirebrook

With Mainline company branding applied over its original Railfreight grey, Class 60 No. 60088 *Buachaille Etive Mor* goes north at Shirebrook with a loaded coal working in September 1996 on what was then a freight-only line from Pye Bridge Junction to Shireoaks, some eighteen months before the re-opening of the passenger station here.

No. 50033 returns to the Western Region

Following attention at Doncaster Works, Class 50 No. 50033 *Glorious* is returned to its home territory courtesy of pilot duty on a Newcastle–Plymouth service. It is seen here powering through Chesterfield in August 1984, while train engine No. 47592 *County of Avon* is behind. (J. M. Walker)

Double-headed 31s on bogie bolsters

A murky day at Chesterfield sees a pair of Class 31s, with No. 31138 leading, take their lengthy train of empty steel bolster wagons across to the Down goods line in preparation to diverge onto the Barrow Hill route at Tapton Junction. Despite the mist, this was in August 1984. (J. M. Walker)

Classic traction at Chinley station

A superb late summer morning at Chinley sees Class 40 No. 40094 heading in the Sheffield direction with a train of empty hoppers. The date was September 1981, and the large-scale withdrawal of these pioneering English Electric Type 4s was yet to come. (V. Hellam)

TransPennine splendour at Chinley

A four-car TransPennine unit makes a splendid sight on the quadruple track section of the Hope Valley route between Chinley and Chinley North Junction as it heads a Manchester–Hull service in September 1981. This section was reduced to two tracks not long afterwards when the area was re-signalled. (V. Hellam)

Sprinter pioneer at Cromford

The pioneer of the Class 150 Sprinter fleet, No. 150001, emerges from Willersley tunnel and into Cromford station in the summer of 1988 with a three-coach Matlock–Derby service on the former Midland Main Line from Manchester. These services now extend to Newark and are typically worked by Class 153 or 156 units.

Peak Forest departure

In this view of Peak Forest on the Chinley–Buxton freight route in June 2016, Class 66 No. 66063 brings some empty hoppers out of the sidings while, on the right, Class 60 No. 60019 *The Railway Magazine* waits on the refuelling point.

HST speeding south at Clay Cross

A clean-looking HST set in uniform original livery powers through Clay Cross on a NE–SW service in June 1983. At this time the HSTs were displacing many Class 45, 46 and 47-hauled services on the Midland route, facilitating the acceleration of timings on the network. (J. M. Walker)

Class 37s gather in Barrow Hill yard

A cluster of DRS Class 37s stands in the yard at Barrow Hill in February 2014. On the left is No. 37422, with No. 37261 heading the line on the right. Class 03 No. 03066 is busy providing brake van rides to visitors while A4 Pacific No. 4464 *Bittern* is just visible at the platform.

Mix-and-match HST passes Lincoln

With a uniform rake of blue-and-grey Mk III coaches, an InterCity-liveried HST power car accelerates a diverted East Coast service through Lincoln station on a Sunday afternoon in January 1986. Bookending the train is another grey-and-yellow power car.

Diverted HST approaches Lincoln

Weekend services on the East Coast Main Line were diverted via Lincoln during January 1986, and here a northbound HST passes Pelham Street Junction level crossing as it approaches the station. Newly delivered Sprinter units stand outside the shed on the left.

No. 25300 heads empty hoppers back to Buxton

A misty afternoon at Great Rocks Junction in April 1983 sees Class 25 No. 25300 drifting down from Peak Forest to Great Rocks with a rake of empty aggregates hoppers. The classic steam-era wagons were synonymous with this route until they were replaced by more modern versions in the late 1980s. (V. Hellam)

Easy load for No. 40141

A rake of empty aggregates hoppers destined for Tunstead drifts down through Peak Forest in the capable hands of Class 40 No. 40141 in April 1983. The Class 40s were not to last much longer on this traffic, with which they had been associated for many years. (V. Hellam)

Grindleford sidings

A telephoto view of the signalbox and sidings at Grindleford, on the Hope Valley route from Sheffield to Manchester. In May 1985, a pair of Class 25s, with No. 25109 nearest the camera, takes a break between duties.

Hope Valley survivor

The well-engineered TransPennine DMUs were built at Swindon and introduced in 1960. Arguably one of the best-looking designs of the era, and originally configured as six-car units, they were a very good substitute for locomotive-haulage on cross-country routes. Here, one of the shortened four-car units speeds through Bamford on a Manchester service in August 1983.

The 'Worksop Whistler' at Bilsthorpe colliery

This special tour visited a number of collieries in the Derbyshire and Nottinghamshire area on 28 June 1992. Here the train is seen after arrival at Bilsthorpe pit with Class 20s Nos 20057 and 20154 on the rear. Sisters Nos 20168 and 20059 are at the other end. The colliery had three years of life ahead of it at this time.

Passenger rarity on the Welbeck Colliery branch

The 'Worksop Whistler' tour of June 1992 is seen here again on its tour of Nottinghamshire and Derbyshire collieries. Here, Nos 20057 and 20154 lead their train towards the pit yard at Welbeck. Motive power for the return leg will be provided by Nos 20168 and 20059 at the other end of the train.

Brush 4 on Piccadilly–Yarmouth run

Making a change from Class 40 motive power, Brush Type 4 No. 47266 brings its Yarmouth train up the grade from Shireoaks and into Worksop on the final Saturday of August 1983. (J. M. Walker)

Featureless 40 on Saturday Yarmouth turn

With nose-end doors plated over and headcode discs removed, Class 40 No. 40058 presents a somewhat sterile appearance as it brings a Manchester–Yarmouth service out of Worksop in September 1983. The lack of visual appeal is not spoiling the enjoyment of the many traction fans on board. (J. M. Walker)

Freight and passenger workings at Lincoln

A recently introduced Class 150 Sprinter waits to depart Lincoln Central with a Birmingham service, while Class 47 No. 47321 passes on the through roads with empty bulk oil tanks from Kingsbury to Immingham in June 1987. Class 47s were the dominant motive power for these services in the late '80s.

Bulk oil empties at Lincoln

One of the most important freight flows through the region to this day is bulk oil, with several trains making a daily journey from Humberside to distribution depots. In 1987, pairs of Class 31s were frequent performers alongside the Brush Type 4s and, in this image, Nos 31202 and 31206 are seen at Lincoln with a return train of empties for Immingham.

Shirebrook before the station rebuilding

In September 1996, Class 58 No. 58024 tows Class 60 No. 60088 through Shirebrook station in the direction of Worksop. This was around eighteen months before the re-opening of the station here as part of the Nottingham–Mansfield–Worksop 'Robin Hood Line' renaissance.

Peak No. 44007 returns to base

After working an earlier mixed freight to Tinsley, original Peak Class 44 No. 44007, one of only three left in service at this time, trundles down the Midland Main Line at Chesterfield on its way back to its home depot of Toton in October 1979. Fellow survivors Nos 44004 and 44008 were the other two still in traffic.

Type 3 line-up at Buxton

This is a view of Buxton's stabling point in August 1992, with a line-up of Railfreight-liveried Class 37s present. At the front of this quartet is No. 37688 *Great Rocks*. The 37s were dependable performers on aggregate trains in the Buxton area for many years.

Double-headed 56 power for Stourton hoppers

This pair of DCR Class 56s, Nos 56311 and 56312, is preparing to work a hopper service out of Peak Forest sidings to Stourton at Leeds in August 2012. This was a relatively unusual traction choice for the aggregates traffic, Class 60s and 66s being the more typical option. (V. Hellam)

Westbound departures at Lincoln

Lincoln station on a June evening in 1987, and there are Crewe-bound trains on either side of the island platform. On the left a recently introduced Class 150 Sprinter prepares to depart, while Class 31 No. 31457 is in charge of 1M77, the daily TPO.

Evening in semaphore city

A June evening in 1987 sees Class 31 No. 31294 threading its way between Lincoln's semaphore signals with an eastbound parcels service. The train will be taking the Sleaford line.

Aggregates on the move at Peak Forest

The hills echo to the sound of Type 4 Sulzer power as Class 47 No. 47227 gets a loaded aggregate train moving from Peak Forest Sidings in June 1988. With no banker attached, the Brush 4 is working hard to shift the substantial load, as Class 37 No. 37207 edges cautiously to a stop with another train, with the hard part yet to come.

Class 45 Peak heads for South Wales at Bamford

Peak Class 45 No. 45003 is seen here on the approach to Bamford on the Hope Valley route with an evening cement working from Tunstead, near Buxton, to Margam in South Wales, in August 1983.

Green Type 4s at Toton

Carrying different variants of their original BR green liveries, Class 47s Nos 47114 *Freightlinerbulk* (nearest the camera) and 47500 *Great Western* stand in the shed yard at Toton depot in 1998.

Back to green for No. 47004

Displaying a fixed four-character headcode panel, Class 47 No. 47004 *Old Oak Common Traction & Rolling Stock Depot* stands on display at Toton depot in August 1998. No. 47004 was allocated to Bescot at the time of this picture, but was later purchased for preservation on the Embsay & Bolton Abbey Railway.

Toton Type 5s

A pair of Brush-built locomotives stands on display at Toton in August 1998. On the left is the first of the re-built Class 47s, No. 57001 *Freightliner Pioneer*, and alongside is Class 60 No. 60006 *Scunthorpe Ironmaster*, which previously carried the name *Great Gable*. The Class 57 began life in the 1960s as D1875.

General Motors Type 5 at Toton

A Class not normally associated with Toton, the 59s first appeared on British metals in the late 1980s, and have enjoyed a lengthy career on aggregates traffic in the South West of England, among other duties. Here the Class pioneer No. 59001 *Yeoman Endeavour* stands outside the shed in August 1998.

Toton depot Open Day, June 1979

Among the locomotives on display at the Toton Open Day in June 1979 was original Peak Class 44 No. 44004 *Great Gable*. Seen here in corporate rail blue, this Peak was in fact repainted in its original green livery in 1980, complete with 'lion and wheel' crest and with nameplate restored. It survives in preservation today.

Celebrity status for No. 44008 at Toton

Among the exhibits at Toton Open Day in June 1979 is original Peak No. 44008 *Penyghent*. Sporting silver buffers and red bufferbeam, the locomotive attracted many visitors keen to take a look in the cab. No. 44008 was a mere twenty years old at the time of this picture, but was already on the brink of withdrawal from BR service.

No. 20071 on display at Toton

In a typically work-stained condition, Class 20 No. 20071 has clearly not received any special attention before being selected for display at Toton's Open Day on Saturday 9 June 1979. This particular locomotive survived another sixteen years in traffic before being scrapped in Glasgow in 1995.

Pioneering livery change for No. 56036

Toton-based Class 56 No. 56036 created headlines in 1979 when it was out-shopped in a new variant of Rail Blue livery featuring an outsized logo and number, with full yellow cabs. The new look was later rolled out to many more locomotives but, in June 1979, when No. 56036 was on display at the Toton Open Day, it was still an attention-grabbing novelty.

Nos 50007 and 56105 on empty steel coils service, Attenborough

Class 50 No. 50007 makes a rare appearance on the regular Washwood Heath (Metro Cammell)–Boston Docks empty steel coils service, and is seen here storming along the section between Trent Junction and Nottingham with No. 56105 behind in May 2014. For good measure a Class 47 is tagging along at the back.

No. 47501 on Nottingham-bound parcels

With the original waiting shelter still *in situ* on the Derby-bound platform, this is Attenborough station in May 1989. Class 47 No. 47501 *Craftsman* speeds towards Nottingham with a parcels service. The footbridge visible here has since been replaced with a higher, lighter structure that will enable overhead electrification wires to pass beneath.

Early Type 2 at Derby Works

One of the early batch of Class 25s, Haymarket-allocated No. 25011 is seen here inside one of the repair shops at Derby Works in August 1978. Although Derby constructed many of these Sulzer-engined Type 2s, this particular example was built at Darlington. Whatever attention it received on this occasion, it was not to last much longer in service, being scrapped at Swindon in 1981.

Green-liveried survivor at Derby

This Class 20, No. 20151, has done well to avoid a repaint into corporate rail blue as late as 1979 and is still carrying its somewhat faded green livery, albeit without any insignia, in this image from July of that year. Complete with grey roof and red buffer beam, the veteran Type 1 trundles past Derby station on a southbound freight in the days when the area behind was occupied by the famous locomotive works.

No. 60081 in Great Western green

Wearing its distinctive and unique green livery, Class 60 No. 60081 *Isambard Kingdom Brunel* approaches Derby off the Burton line with empty steel bolster wagons for Teesside in August 2002. It carried the name of the great engineer for a further seven years.

Corus Steel No. 60033 at Derby

Another livery variant is displayed on Class 60 No. 60033 *Tees Steel Express*, seen here passing Derby with a mix of empty and loaded wagons in Corus Steel's pale grey colours in the summer of 2002. Steel coil is a major freight flow through this East Midlands hub.

Diverted Coatbridge containers pass Attenborough Junction

Flood damage on the West Coast Main Line north of Carlisle in February 2016 caused the diversion of numerous trains, including this container service from Daventry, which will take a circuitous route to reach its destination at Glasgow. Class 66 No. 66551 heads towards Nottingham with this Sunday-only diagram, which will arrive at Coatbridge in the early hours of Monday morning.

No. 66079 waits for a Class 170 unit, Attenborough Junction

No. 66079 waits for the right-away to cross Attenborough Junction and take the high level line to its home base at Toton, as the source of the hold-up, a Class 170 Turbostar unit, passes with a service from Birmingham to Nottingham in the summer of 2014. The route to Trent Junction goes straight ahead here.

Type 1 power for St Pancras special

This is the Midland Main Line at Newton Harcourt, south of Leicester. Class 20s Nos 20228 and 20145 have cleared Wigston Junction and are picking up speed with a special bound for St Pancras in May 1989.

Unusual motive power for the Midland Main Line

Heading north from Market Harborough towards Leicester, a pair of Southern Region Class 33s, Nos 33021 and 33022, lead 1T10, a special Hertfordshire Railtours passenger service from St Pancras, at Newton Harcourt in May 1989.

No. 66138 meets No. 60074, Attenborough

The Midland Main Line between Nottingham and Trent Junction is one of the most intensively used stretches in the country, with passenger and freight services competing for paths throughout the day. Here No. 66138 heads towards Trent on a light engine move while, through the haze, No. 60074 can be seen approaching with an empty bulk oil train bound for Humberside.

A busy scene at Attenborough Junction

The freight-only chord to Meadow Lane Junction and thence Toton yard diverges from the main Nottingham–Trent line here at Attenborough Junction. Awaiting a path across the junction on the left, No. 66508 stands with a ballast cleaning train destined for Doncaster, while HST No. 43046 approaches with an evening St Pancras service.

No. 67024 makes way for a celebrity at Derby

Class 67 No. 67024 has been taken off the stock of a Settle & Carlisle excursion at Derby in this image from a bright December morning in 2013. Deltic D9009 *Alycidon*, which has arrived light engine from Barrow Hill, waits to take over for the journey to the north.

East Coast racehorse on the Great Central

On what would historically have been very much foreign territory for the Class, Deltic D9009 *Alycidon* makes a guest appearance at Loughborough's Central station in the summer of 2010. In common with many diesels of its era, D9009 has now been in preservation for many more years than it was in BR service.

No. 20102 at Toton depot

The traction maintenance depot at Toton, the largest on the BR network, was long associated with the Class 20s, but the number in active service was dwindling by the time this image was captured in the summer of 1991. No. 20102 stands outside its home base on 13 July.

Toton Type 1s in profile

Once such a common sight at depots throughout the region, the Class 20s at one time numbered over 200 examples. Here two of Toton's allocation are seen in profile at their home base in the summer of 1992, a time at which their numbers began to diminish.

Helping hand for No. 56054 at Burton upon Trent

As the flags fly over the nearby brewery, Class 20s Nos 20159 and 20157 haul 'dead' No. 56054 past Burton's island platform and towards the nearby stabling point in July 1979. Later named *British Steel Llanwern*, No. 56054 was scrapped in 2011.

Class 31s head bulk oil at Barrow

Carrying variants of the same livery – one with red stripe and one without – Class 31s Nos 31319 and 31188 power through Barrow-on-Soar in Leicestershire with a southbound bulk oil working in September 1989.

Lightweight load for No. 66072

This is Sandiacre, to the north of Toton depot; Class 66 No. 66072 passes the site of the former Stapleford & Sandiacre station with a short load of open spoil wagons on a Saturday morning in April 2001.

No. 66150 on loaded coal at Sandiacre

A bright afternoon in September 2002 sees EWS Class 66 No. 66150 approaching Stapleford & Sandiacre on the Erewash Valley main line with a loaded MGR train from one of the Nottinghamshire collieries.

Prototype Metro-Cammell unit at Beeston

This is the second of the two prototype aluminium-bodied Class 151 diesel units built by Metro-Cammell in 1987 for evaluation on the BR network. Here No. 151002 pauses at Beeston while working a Derby–Nottingham service in the summer of that year.

Prototype Sprinter passes Attenborough

A hazy summer's day at Attenborough in 1989 sees prototype Class 150 Sprinter No. 154002, formerly No. 150002, heading towards Derby on a service from Nottingham to Crewe.

Ex-works Peak on show at Derby

This is Derby locomotive works, with immaculate Peak Class 46 No. 46007 basking in the August sunshine during the 1978 Open Day. This would be the last full overhaul and repaint for this particular locomotive, which was withdrawn only four years later.

Derby Works Open Day, 1978

This is a bird's eye view of some of the exhibits on display at Derby's open day in August 1978. Visiting from Doncaster is newly built No. 56045, while Crewe's HST power car W43121 is also on show. Behind is Derby's own Peak No. 45044.

Alexander Fleming on Humber oil tanks

This is Attenborough station in the summer of 1993. The waiting shelter, light signal and footbridge have all been replaced in the intervening years, and further transformation will come when overhead electrification reaches Nottingham in 2019. Here No. 60014 *Alexander Fleming*, with appropriate petroleum sector branding, heads the Kingsbury–Humber empty oil tanks.

No. 58041 on empty MGR return trip

A hazy 26 May 1992 sees Class 58 No. 58041 *Ratcliffe Power Station* passing Attenborough with empty hoppers returning to one of the region's collieries. The service had probably originated at the same power station. Built at Doncaster Works, the locomotive is carrying its second colour scheme of Railfreight Coal Sector grey.

HST unit No. 43049 approaches Stoke Tunnel

The overhead electrification masts had yet to appear on this stretch of the East Coast Main Line in the summer of 1986, when HST unit No. 43049 was caught speeding towards King's Cross on the approach to Stoke Tunnel, south of Grantham.

Northbound HST at Stoke Tunnel

An InterCity-liveried HST set, with power car No. 43079 leading, bursts out of Stoke Tunnel's northern portal with a King's Cross–Edinburgh service in the summer of 1986. This was shortly before the overhead electrification masts started to go up.

Up on the jacks at Toton

A veil of diesel fumes drifts above Class 56 No. 56010, which is receiving attention inside the shed at Toton in September 1992. One of the original Romanian-built examples, this loco's first home base was Tinsley. (J. M. Walker)

Type 5 line-up at Toton

Three of the depot's veteran Type 1s keep company with a trio of relatively new arrivals in the form of Class 58s Nos 58002, 58027 and 58032 at Toton in August 1988. No. 58002 sports the new-look Coal Sector grey livery with small cab front numerals. Its partners are in as-built condition. (J. M. Walker)

Brush pair in Railfreight grey at Toton

Thirty years of design evolution separates these two Brush machines – on the left is Class 31 No. 31233, alongside newly delivered No. 60077 *Canisp*, seen here at Toton depot in September 1992. The sturdy Type 2 has, however, outlived its far newer compatriot and still serves as part of the Network Rail departmental fleet.

Class 56s predominate at Toton

Wearing Railfreight Coal Sector livery, Class 56s Nos 56082 and 56084, both Doncaster-built examples, stand at Toton in September 1992. In the background is one of the original Romanian-built imports, No. 56006, which retains all-over blue livery. Toton was taking delivery of greater numbers of Class 60 locomotives at this time, and more Class 56s were finding themselves stored out of service.

Humble duty for high speed Brush Type 4

One of a small batch of 100-mph-rated Class 47s, No. 47973 *Derby Evening Telegraph* is seen here at Derby on a rake of engineers' wagons on 15 June 1993. This locomotive previously carried a different name linked to the region, *Midland Counties Railway 150 1839–1989*. After carrying no fewer than four previous identities – D1614, 47034, 47561 and 97561 – No. 47973 lasted only a further four years in service before being scrapped at Crewe in 1997.

Derby stabling point

At least half a dozen Class 31s, some of which are withdrawn, are present at Derby's stabling point in June 1993. In the foreground, Class 47 No. 47528 *The Queen's Own Mercian Yeomanry* will shortly move off to take charge of a TPO service.

Nos 20026 and 20085 on engineering duty, Long Eaton

Class 20s Nos 20026 and 20085 are seen here on the Erewash Valley line, which runs from Clay Cross to Trent Junction via Toton Yard. On the section between Toton and Trent is Long Eaton Town level crossing, site of the former passenger station, and where engineering work was taking place on a rather misty 6 November 1988. There are many characteristic lattice design footbridges on this section of line.

Return of the 'Jolly Fisherman'

One of the popular summer Saturday Skegness services rolls into Nottingham station on its return leg to Derby on 1 July 1993. Class 20s Nos 20066 and 20138, the latter in 'large logo' grey livery, are in charge. This diagram was a traditional Class 20 turn.

HST unit No. 43079 goes south from Leicester

HST unit No. 43079 has left the suburbs of Leicester behind and is passing Newton Harcourt on its way to London St Pancras on a service from Sheffield in May 1989. This particular power car was still in service over twenty-five years later, as a member of the First Great Western fleet.

Cooling towers loom large at East Midlands Parkway

The giant cooling towers of Ratcliffe-on-Soar power station dominate the platforms at East Midlands Parkway as a London-bound HST slows for its stop in June 2009. Leading power car is No. 43048 *T.C.B. Miller MBE*, named after the HST's original chief engineer.

Re-ballasting on the Midland Main Line

The Midland Main Line between Nottingham and Trent Junction was closed for re-ballasting work in February 2013. Here newly repainted DB Schenker Class 60s Nos 60010 and 60017 are in charge of disposal and replenishment at Attenborough.

No. 66413 on Sunday ballast duty

In DRS blue livery, but wearing Freightliner ID, No. 66413 approaches Barton Lane between Trent Junction and Nottingham with a Sunday ballast trip from Toton to Beeston South in January 2016. The wall in the foreground is part of the Trent flood defence infrastructure.

No. 25140 on freight at Burton

This July 1979 picture shows Class 25 No. 25140 heading north at Burton-on-Trent with a freight working. The barren island platform at Burton has since been extensively landscaped. The Sulzer Type 2 was withdrawn in 1983 and dismantled at Swindon.

Lightweight load for No. 47289

Carrying Railfreight Distribution sector livery, Class 47 No. 47289 heads south on the Midland Main Line at Barrow-on-Soar with a short train of open wagons in September 1989.

Nos 20196 and 20084 on display at Nottingham station

As part of celebrations to mark the 150th anniversary of the Midland Counties Railway, which was the first company to construct a line through the city, a number of locomotives were displayed at Nottingham station in June 1989. Among them was Class 20 No. 20196, seen here with sister No. 20084.

Brand-new HST at Nottingham

An immaculate new HST set, with unit No. 254035 leading, stands at Nottingham after arriving on a test run from Derby in August 1982. The HSTs were still mainly operating over the East Coast and Western Region main lines at this time, but were starting to appear on cross-country services through the Midlands. (J. M. Walker)

New livery for No. 56091 at Toton

Resplendent in its new maroon-and-yellow EWS colours, Doncaster-built Class 56 No. 56091 *Stanton* stands in the shed yard at Toton on the occasion of the Open Weekend of August 1998. Behind is the equally immaculate No. 37417.

No. 56049 meets the new arrival at Toton

This is Toton depot in July 1991, and No. 56049 is one of more than thirty examples of the Class 'on shed' that day. Stealing into the picture on the right is newly built Brush Type 5 No. 60040, one of just two present. The numbers would soon swing in favour of the Loughborough-built machines.

Freightliner Crusader at Derby

Class 57 No. 57010 *Freightliner Crusader* takes a container service south through Derby in August 2002. Built at Loughborough's Brush foundry, this locomotive was previously Class 47 No. 47231. In Class 57 guise it is powered by a General Motors engine and Class 56 traction motors. The green-and-yellow livery later gave way to DRS blue.

Light engine quintet at Derby

Class 60 No. 60046 *William Wilberforce* pauses at Derby during a light engine transit from Toton to Bescot depot in August 2002. On tow behind are two more Class 60s and a pair of Class 66s.

Decades of design evolution at Derby

Derby station in 2004, and one of the relatively new General Motors Class 66s heads south with empty coal hoppers on the avoiding lines. Standing in a siding behind, preserved Peak No. 45112 presents a contrasting but, one could argue, more characterful profile.

Class 222 and 66 at Derby

Freightliner's No. 66952, one of seven of the 66/9 sub-class, takes a northbound hopper train past Derby station in October 2009 as a St Pancras service waits to depart Platform 6 with Class 222 unit No. 222009. No. 66952 was modified from the standard type to achieve reduced exhaust emissions.

Class 150 approaches Beeston

In as-delivered condition, Class 150 Sprinter No. 150150 slows for its Beeston stop on a service from Lincoln to Crewe in July 1987. This was one of the first services in the area to convert to Class 150 operation.

Unique Type 4 on display at Nottingham

Carrying the number 97561, and in distinctive maroon livery with full yellow ends, Brush Type 4 *Midland Counties Railway 150 1839–1989* stands on display at Nottingham station in June 1989, in connection with celebrations commemorating the events after which it is named. Shortly afterwards it was renumbered as 47973, though initially it retained the name.

Engineer's duty for Nos 20106 and 20138

Heading further south on the Midland Main Line, this is Barrow-on-Soar on the four-track section between Leicester and Loughborough. In the days before Barrow's passenger station was re-opened close to this spot, Nos 20106 and 20138 head a ballast working in September 1989.

No. 20902 applies the weedkiller at Barrow

Sporting grey Hunslet-Barclay livery, No. 20902 *Lorna* goes south at Barrow-on-Soar with a weed-killing service in September 1989. Sister No. 20906 was on the rear of the train. No. 20902 was originally D8060 and then No. 20060 before being renumbered in the 20/9 series. The locomotive was cut up in 2011.

66s north and south at Toton

In this image from September 2002, EWS Class 66s Nos 66155 and 66150 pass, with empty and full coal workings respectively, at the north end of Toton yard. No. 66155 has charge of the newer generation high-capacity hoppers while No. 66150 hauls a rake of the original 30-tonne MGR wagons.

Class 20s await their fate

These sidings at Sandiacre, to the north of Toton yard, were used for storing a number of withdrawn Class 20s in the early 1990s, and in this view there are around nine examples of the Type 1 visible. There were many more stored at Toton itself. This image dates from March 1992.

Super power for the 'Northern Belle'

The empty coaching stock of the 'Northern Belle' Pullman service heads away from Nottingham on a test run in September 2016. Class 68 No. 68001 *Evolution* leads the way, with sister No. 68022 *Resolution* at the rear, destination York via Derby.

Nos 20052 and 20004 on engineering duty, Attenborough

Heading from Nottingham towards Toton, this pair of Class 20s was caught on camera approaching Attenborough station in May 1989 with a train of recovered track and ballast hoppers. Class 20s were a popular choice on this type of working in and around the Toton area.

Vintage Type 4 line-up at Toton

The Open Weekend at Toton in August 1998 brought many preserved locomotives to the site, providing an opportunity to see classes not normally associated with the depot, including those seen here. Former Western Region machines No. 50015 *Valiant*, D1023 *Western Fusilier* and D444 *Exeter* line up in the sunshine on the south side of the shed.

Type 5 storage facility

A lengthy line of withdrawn Class 60s, sporting a range of fading liveries, stands at Toton in May 2016. At twenty-four locomotives in total, the line of redundant Type 5s stretches for almost half a kilometre alongside the yard. Several years after they were first put in storage here, their fate remains unclear.

Peaks receive attention at Derby Works

The workshops at Derby are seen here with Sulzer Type 4s Nos 45126, 45148 and 45117 in March 1985. All three were released back to traffic after repair, though their time was fast running out. (J. M. Walker)

37s power through Long Eaton

A rainy Saturday morning at Long Eaton in September 2016 sees a Matlock–Newark service pausing at the platform as Class 37s Nos 37608 and 37611 power through on a Network Rail test train, running as 1Z18 from Peterborough to Derby.

Royal Mail top'n'tail at Derby

Class 47 No. 47528 *The Queen's Own Mercian Yeomanry* waits for No. 08536 to attach a single Royal Mail van at Derby in June 1993. The Class 08 was subsequently withdrawn and retained at Derby for spare parts.

Peak No. 45044 awaits attention at Derby Works

A regular at Derby Works, this particular Peak, No. 45044, was in resplendent ex-works condition at the time of the 1978 Open Day; however, just a year later in September 1979, it looks here very much the daily workhorse as it awaits repair.

East Coast passenger duty for No. 31421

This is the north end of Stoke Tunnel, around 10 miles south of Grantham on the East Coast Main Line. On a beautiful late summer's day in September 1986, No. 31421 bursts into the sunlight with a semi-fast passenger service. This was shortly before electrification of the route here.

Modified HST on Grand Central service at Grantham

HST power cars operated by Grand Central on the Sunderland–King's Cross route are all from the batch once modified to act as Driving Van Trailers, or DVTs, on the East Coast route; hence they feature the buffers and exposed drawbar gear not seen on the original design. This example, No. 43465, is passing Grantham with a southbound service in September 2016.

Bulk oil tanks on the move at Attenborough

No doubt heading for Humberside, a relatively short train of empty oil tanks heads through Attenborough in June 1989. Motive power is provided by Class 47 No. 47374. Several daily loaded oil trains, and their empty counterparts, operate over this section of the Midland Main Line six days a week, though the Brush Type 4s have been superseded by their somewhat newer cousins, the Class 60s.

No. 20196 at Nottingham

Toton-based Class 20 No. 20196 heads up a line of locomotives on display at Nottingham station in June 1989 in conjunction with 150-year anniversary celebrations for the Nottingham–Derby route.

The Peak that escaped total destruction

The black-and-white measurement tape attached to the leading edge of Peak No. 46023 indicates that this was one of the candidate locomotives for a controlled collision test, designed to prove the safety of nuclear flask wagons. In a highly publicised event, sister No. 46009 hurtled to oblivion and No. 023 was reprieved. It is seen here at Toton depot in March 1985. (J. M. Walker)

Classic traction at Toton depot

This is Toton depot in March 1985, with a selection of classic diesel traction present. Peak No. 45074 stands with Sulzer stable mate No. 25185, while Class 56s Nos 56070 and 56084 are also in attendance. The Class 25 is also carrying its original number, D7535. (J. M. Walker)

Mountsorrel-bound at Leicester

EWS-liveried Class 66 No. 66068 goes north through Leicester with a rake of refurbished aggregate hoppers in their new pale grey 'Tarmac' colours in August 2016. A large number of freight workings pass through Leicester on a daily basis, bound for the aggregate terminal at Mountsorrel near Loughborough. This one has originated at Elstow, further south on the Midland Main Line.

No. 66591 on Felixstowe container service at Leicester

Freightliner's No. 66591 is held at signals on the platform avoiding lines at Leicester station while heading a container service returning to the port of Felixstowe in August 2016. This service originated at Freightliner's Lawley Street terminal in Birmingham and will take the Stamford line at Syston Junction as it makes its way east.

Silver Jubilee look for No. 47580

A Stratford-on-Avon–Skegness returning excursion passes Attenborough in April 2016. Sporting a design first seen in 1977, Union Jack-adorned Class 47 No. 47580 *County of Essex* is trailing the coaching stock. Sister No. 47760 was leading.

No. 60099 on Humber–Kingsbury tanks

Passing Barton Lane level crossing, north of Trent Junction, Tata Steel-liveried Class 60 No. 60099 heads the Humber Refinery–Kingsbury bulk oil tanks in April 2015. Most of the oil trains on this route are destined for the distribution depot to the south of Tamworth in Warwickshire.

Crompton power for Coalville Open Day

In the heart of rural Leicestershire, Class 33 No. 33058 constitutes rare motive power for a special from London Euston, destined for the Open Day at Coalville in June 1989. Here the train, named 'The Coalville Cobbler', approaches a foot crossing at Merry Lees.

Coalville Open Day DMU

On what is normally a freight-only line, this DMU is seen at Merry Lees in Leicestershire with a special shuttle service, taking visitors from Leicester station to the Coalville Open Day on 11 June 1989.

Resplendent Class 20s at Derby

Type 1 survivors Nos 20132 and 20118 stand in the late summer sunshine at Derby in September 2014. A number of these diesel pioneers have survived into the twenty-first century and are deployed on a variety of engineer's duties. This pair looks particularly smart in Railfreight grey livery – a real credit to those who have restored and maintained them over the years.

Aggregate return trip for No. 66019

The elegant platform canopies of Melton Mowbray's beautifully preserved station frame EWS-liveried Class 66 No. 66019 as it snakes out of the Down goods loop with a train of empty aggregate wagons returning to Mountsorrel near Loughborough in June 2016. This is a heavily used cross-country freight route.

Beeston engineer's trip for No. 67029 *Royal Diamond*

A short set of rail-carrying wagons forms the load for Class 67 No. 67029 *Royal Diamond* as it heads towards Beeston in June 2016. The locomotive was named in 2007 on the occasion of HM the Queen's Diamond wedding anniversary.

Class 68s curve through Trent Junction

A top-and-tail combination of Class 68s takes the stock of the 'Northern Belle' Pullman set through the reverse curves at Trent East Junction in September 2016. No. 68001 *Evolution* is at the front, with No. 68022 *Resolution* behind. The train is about to pass beneath the high-level line from Trent Junction to Toton Yard.

Virgin HST and Turbostar unit at Derby

This is Derby station in the summer of 2004, and a Virgin-liveried HST unit waits to depart with a NE–SW service, while a Class 170 Turbostar has just arrived in the adjacent platform. The Class 170 units were operating some services to St Pancras at this time, prior to the arrival of the Meridian Class 222 units.

No. 58001 on test at Derby

Pioneer Doncaster-built Type 5 No. 58001 is seen here at Derby in early 1983 at the head of a test train comprising a rake of Research Technical Centre coaching stock. A profusion of cabling takes all the necessary performance data from the locomotive back to the analysts. (J. M. Walker)

Electric and diesel power at Grantham

The busy junction of Grantham sees plenty of electric- and diesel-hauled traffic as this scene from September 2016 demonstrates, with a Leeds–King's Cross service standing at Platform 1. Meanwhile, a pair of Freightliner's Class 66s, Nos 66517 and 66502, power a northbound container service, which has originated at Felixstowe.

Class 91 applies the brakes at Grantham

A cloud of brake dust follows Class 91 No. 91121 as it slows for its stop at Grantham while working the 10.38 London King's Cross–Leeds service. These trains are always configured with the 6,300-hp locomotive at the north end and a Driving Van Trailer, or DVT, at the south, or London, end of the train. The entire nine-coach ensemble is also known as an InterCity 225.

Classic traction line-up at Toton depot

Seen from inside the depot building, a collection of classic motive power lines up on the occasion of the Open Weekend at Toton in August 1998. The Peak and Class 20 are on familiar territory; the Class 40, Warship and Deltic less so. This was the last time that Toton opened its doors to the public.

New livery for No. 58050

The last of Doncaster's batch of Class 58s, and indeed the last locomotive ever built at the famous 'plant', No. 58050 stands in its new maroon-and-yellow EWS livery at Toton depot in August 1998. It had carried the name *Toton Traction Depot* for over ten years at this point. Although by no means a veteran, and arguably a candidate for the National Collection, it was withdrawn in 2002 and later exported to Spain.

No. 47168 performs rescue duties at Burton

Class 47 No. 47168 leads failed partner No. 47312 on a very mixed collection of freight vehicles at Burton upon Trent in July 1979. Later renumbered as 47572, and named *Ely Cathedral*, No. 47168 was withdrawn and scrapped twenty years later in 1999.

No. 47379 on merry-go-round hoppers, Burton upon Trent

Coal flows across the East Midlands have changed markedly since July 1979, when this Class 47 was captured turning on the power at Burton upon Trent while heading a southbound merry-go-round service. Its destination could well be nearby Drakelow power station.

Classic traction line-up at Leicester depot

Leicester's UK Rail Leasing depot plays host to a line-up of classic diesel traction in a scene that could almost represent the 1970s – however, this is 2016 and it is still possible to see members of Classes 37, 47 and 56 'on shed'. On the left a pair of Rail Operations Group 37s, Nos 37884 and 37800, stand in front of a quartet of 56s, with Brush Type 4 Nos 47843 and 47812 alongside.

Containers pass Stamford

The stonework and canopies of Stamford's station are undergoing much-deserved restoration as Freightliner's Class 66 No. 66565 takes a Birmingham Lawley Street–Felixstowe container service through in September 2016. This busy freight route sees a lot of traffic to and from the Suffolk port, much of it destined for or originating in the Midlands.

No. 37602 on departmental duty at Long Eaton

Class 37 No. 37602, the original D6782, approaches the site of the former Long Eaton Town station, on the Erewash Valley route between Toton Yard and Trent Junction. With No. 37610 on the rear, it is heading a Network Rail trip from Longsight TMD to Derby in the summer of 2016.

No. 37025 heads Network Rail set through Attenborough

Split-headcode survivor No. 37025 is seen here propelling the Network Rail inspection train through Attenborough and towards Trent Junction in April 2016. On this occasion the trip had originated at Peterborough and would terminate at Derby.

Latest generation motive power on container service

One of the fleet of American-built 'Powerhaul' series Class 70 Co-Co diesels, No. 70010, heads through Derby station in June 2016 with a lengthy container service that has originated at Southampton. Its destination is Stourton, just outside Leeds. These 3,690 hp machines first arrived in Britain in 2009.

Powerhaul Class 70 meets Brush survivor

They both carry green and yellow livery, but there the resemblance ends: fifty years of technological evolution separate Freightliner's No. 70010 and veteran Brush Type 2 No. 31452, seen here at Derby in June 2016. The Class 31 was built at Loughborough in 1961 as D5809, and later carried the number 31279, assuming its current identity in 1984.